Franky and the Worry Bees

By
Regine Muradian, PsyD

Illustrated By
Timna Green

Franky and The Worry Bees

By
Regine Muradian, PsyD

Illustrated By
Timna Green

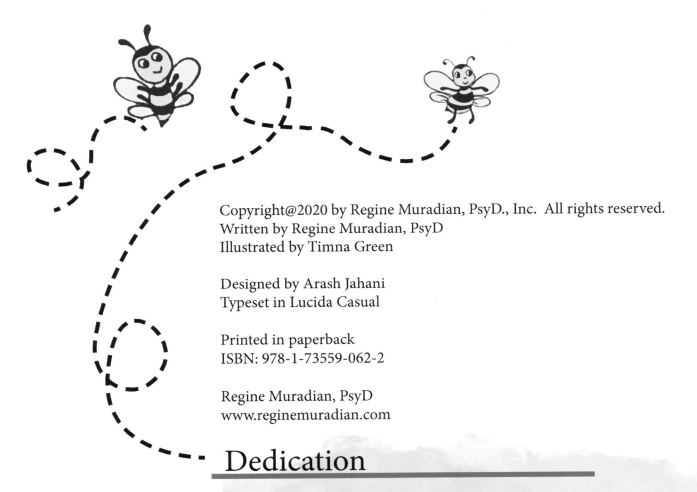

Copyright@2020 by Regine Muradian, PsyD., Inc. All rights reserved.
Written by Regine Muradian, PsyD
Illustrated by Timna Green

Designed by Arash Jahani
Typeset in Lucida Casual

Printed in paperback
ISBN: 978-1-73559-062-2

Regine Muradian, PsyD
www.reginemuradian.com

Dedication

To my three wonderful children Marina, Lori, and A.J.: You inspire me every day. You have taught me patience and that love has no limits. To my best friend and husband Shant: Thank you for supporting me and encouraging me to be the best I can be.

To my incredible, hard-working clients: You motivate me daily. Watching you grow and combat your stressors gives me joy in the work we do together. Thank you for your support and patience.

The Worry Bees Bubble

Franky was worried. And, when he was worried, he could hear the worry bees buzzing in his head. He decided to ask his mom about it. "Mom, when I start worrying, I can almost hear this buzzing sound in my head," he said.

His mom laughed. "I know what that is. It's the worry bees. They can show up at anytime and anywhere. They are a part of you. It's okay, in fact it's even useful or helpful to have them, as long as you stay in control of them."

"Do you have them?" Franky asked.

"I sure do," his mom answered. Sometimes it's helpful to feel worried, but if the buzzing gets too loud it can often make you feel sad or frustrated."

"They just seem to get LOUDER and LOUDER," Franky said.

"Yes, I know! I feel that way too sometimes," she said.

"When was the first time you heard them?" his mom asked. "Last year when I was in 2nd grade. I felt like the bees were buzzing in my head all the time. It didn't feel good. I wanted them to go away, but they didn't. They caused me problems at school, at home, and with my friends," Franky said.

"Yes, they are really loud sometimes. It's hard to quiet them down," she said.

"You're right. Once they started, Mom, they wouldn't stop. There was a constant buzzing sound that made me think about all the things I could not do well. I was so tired of it. I needed it to go away!" exclaimed Franky.

Franky continued. "My worry bees got so loud that I felt like I was starting to disappear. They had taken over! The bubble around me became so big because of my worries that I was floating inside it. Does that happen to you sometimes? What do the buzzing bees tell you to worry about?"

"Yes, dear. My buzzing bees tell me I'm not a good enough mom because I'm always so busy with work. They also tell me that I'm not able to do certain things, come to think of it, those buzzing bees are very negative!" said his mom.

His mom continued, "Once the buzzing sound from the bees finds its way into your head, you feel like it won't go away. It's like it's trapped in your mind and you try so hard to get it out, but you feel like you can't. Then you start believing these negative thoughts and give in to them. These feelings may stop you also from playing with your friends sometimes. "You know, YOU can decide it's time to make the worry bees disappear. You can let them go by creating a new bubble with positive thoughts that YOU CAN CONTROL."

"I don't think I understand. How can I do that, Mom? How can I control them?" Franky asked. "We all have different kinds of worry bees. It's normal to feel you are the only one with them, but you are not. Let me explain step-by-step how you can get them under control," she said.

"Did you make your worry bees disappear, Mom?" Franky asked. His mom replied. "I didn't make them disappear completely, but I learned how to control them. I learned how to make myself happier, feel better, and not give in to the buzzing sound. My first step was to write down the names of all the people who loved and supported me."

"That's a good idea, Mom. You and Dad would be on my list," said Franky.

"That makes me happy to hear," said his mom. "Making this list is a nice reminder of people I could go to for help or to talk to when I felt the buzzing sound. Franky, why don't you spend some time thinking about and writing out a list of people you can depend on."

F ranky thought about his list very carefully. He wrote down quite a few names. The list had his family members like his dad, his mom, his grandma, and his grandpa. His list also had quite a few friends and his 3rd grade teacher.

When he was done, his mom asked, "What is the biggest worry you have and when do you have it?"

Franky said, "A lot of my worries revolve around things that happen at school. I'm always worried about raising my hand in class. I worry about talking to anyone on the playground because I feel shy. I worry when I have to take a test too."

"Yes, I can understand that. I used to feel that way about tests when I was younger," said his mom. "How did it feel when the worry bees showed up?"

Franky continued. "When the worry bees showed up, it felt like a big cloud of buzzing bees just sitting over my shoulder. Lots of times it made me want to give up on whatever I was doing. Sometimes the buzzing sound became so loud that I wanted to leave the classroom. I started getting stomach aches and other uncomfortable feelings."

"We should have talked about this before, Franky. I promise you that there are ways for you to stop that buzzing," said his mom.

Franky continued to explain. "The worry bees often told me to look around the classroom and see what everyone else was doing. They made me feel bad. They made it seem like I was the only one having trouble with the test or work we had to do in class! The bees felt so close I could hear what each bee was telling me."

H is mom said, "When the worry bees start buzzing at school, you have a choice to listen or just send them away. They will come and go, but you can control the buzzing sound so it's not so loud."

As Franky and his mom were talking over breakfast, his dad walked in. "We're talking about the worry bees, come join us!" Franky's mom said to his dad.

Franky's dad smiled. "I know what those worry bees are! When I was your age, Franky, mine showed up when I was at home. They loved to come buzzing when I started homework. I usually found every excuse not to do it. Some people call this "procrastination" or being "lazy." I didn't like hearing those words because I knew that wasn't true about me. It was actually the worry bees that were slowing my progress."

"That's exactly what happens to me, Dad!" exclaimed Franky. "When they start their buzzing I usually feel that no one understands me or how I feel. It's hard for others to understand since I am the only one who hears the buzzing sounds. Though the sounds aren't real, they make me feel like they are very real."

Buzzz...

Franky was surprised that even his mom and dad had these buzzing sounds! He wondered what all of their buzzing sounds were. His worry bees told him that he should do anything instead of math, reading, or writing. The worry bees often said that he should hurry through his homework, since he would not do well on it anyway.

DOG

Now that Franky has learned quite a few lessons about how to control his worry bees he wants to speak directly to you. He wants to help you control your worry bees!

Franky says... "Remember before, when my mom said I had a choice. Going ahead and doing my homework was one way that I chose not to listen to the buzzzing sounds anymore. YOU have a choice too, and I know you can do this. Just try!"

I can do this!

Franky has some more tips for you. "Once the worry bees arrived and started buzzing one thing that helped me was to take a deep breath through my nose and blow out through my mouth. This helped me to relax. Then, I would set a timer for fifteen minutes and do my work during that time. When the timer rang, I got up and took a break for five minutes. Doing this helps letting go of the worry bees and creating your own happy bubble with good thoughts."

Franky says... "Bedtime was my worry bees' favorite time to show up. I wondered why they loved nighttime so much. What do you think?"

Franky continues... "One thought I had was how quiet it was at night. I was in bed and nothing was happening around me. So, at night, there were no distractions, no noises, and nothing to prevent me from listening--just silence. It was the perfect time for the worry bees to come since they knew I would listen."

Franky says... "The worry bees loved nighttime because that's when they knew I would hear them LOUD and CLEAR. Do you remember worry bees happening in class during your tests, reading, or quiet time? Do you remember that they sounded louder than when you were playing at recess? Yes, exactly! That's when they love to show up. So what are YOU going to do? You've read how they come and what you can do to let them go. I hope my ideas will help you."

Franky summarizes... "I am so proud that you were able to complete and create your own bubble of positive thoughts. You can be as creative as you want and draw your own bubbles. Paste them in your notebook or your bedroom as positive reminders.

For example, I feel so good when I think of myself playing soccer. The positive thoughts make me feel good and it will help you too. The more you repeat the positive thoughts the less buzzing you will hear. I know you will handle your worry bees. Take the time and do the work. I know you can do this! Thank you for letting me share my story."

Activity:

You can photocopy this page and use as a daily exercise. Write down in the bees bubble the things you worry about. In the empty bubble the opposite of your worries. For example: "I can't do this" goes in the bees bubble and "I can do this" goes into the empty bubble. Repeat your positives bubble everyday.

Dr. Regine is a children's author and child/adolescent clinical psychologist in Southern California. She has over ten years' experience as a clinician, speaker and parent expert. When not writing, she enjoys spending time with her three children and husband. Dr. Regine enjoys hiking, cooking, the ocean, and relaxing with a good book.

Please visit www.reginemuradian.com to learn more and stay updated with new and upcoming books.

Timna Green is an Israeli children's book illustrator. She enjoys illustrating books that incite fantasy and imagination. She enjoys bringing stories to life and creating a world where anything is possible.

CPSIA information can be obtained
at www.ICGtesting.com
Printed in the USA
LVHW072357230521
688297LV00001B/11

* 9 7 8 1 7 3 5 5 9 0 6 2 2 *